Contents

About the Author

Ian Baxter is a military historian who specialises in German twentieth-century military history. He has written more than seventy books, including *Poland: The Eighteen-Day Victory March*; *Panzers in North Africa*; *The Waffen-SS Ardennes Offensive*; *The Western Campaign*; *The 12th SS Panzer Division Hitlerjugend*; *Waffen-SS on the Western Front*; *Waffen-SS on the Eastern Front*; *The Red Army at Stalingrad*; *Elite German Forces of World War II*; *Armoured Warfare: German Tanks of World War II*; *Blitzkrieg*; *Panzer Divisions at War*; *German Armoured Vehicles of World War Two*; *Last Two Years of the Waffen-SS at War*; *German Soldier Uniforms and Insignia*; *German Guns of the Third Reich*; *From Retreat to Defeat: The Last Years of the German Army at War 1943–45* and, most recently, *The Sixth Army and the Road to Stalingrad*.

He has written over a hundred articles, including 'Last days of Hitler', 'Wolf's Lair', 'The Story of the V1 and V2 Rocket Programme', 'Secret Aircraft of World War Two', 'Rommel at Tobruk', 'Hitler's War with his Generals', 'Secret British Plans to Assassinate Hitler', 'The SS at Arnhem', 'Hitlerjugend', 'Battle of Caen 1944', 'Gebirgsjäger at War', 'Panzer Crews', 'Hitlerjugend Guerrillas', 'Last Battles in the East', 'The Battle of Berlin' and many more.

He has also reviewed numerous military studies for publication, supplied thousands of photographs and important documents to various publishers and film production companies worldwide, and he lectures to schools, colleges and universities throughout the United Kingdom and the Republic of Ireland.

IMAGES OF WAR

HITLER'S HOLOCAUST IN UKRAINE 1941–44

RARE PHOTOGRAPHS FROM WARTIME ARCHIVES

Ian Baxter

Pen & Sword
MILITARY

First published in Great Britain in 2025 by
PEN & SWORD MILITARY
an imprint of Pen & Sword Books Ltd
Yorkshire – Philadelphia

ISBN 978-1-03611-238-7

A CIP catalogue record for this book is available from the British Library.

Typeset by Concept, Huddersfield, West Yorkshire, HD4 5JL.
Printed and bound in England by CPI Group (UK) Ltd, Croydon, CR0 4YY.

The Publisher's authorised representative in the EU for product safety is Authorised Rep Compliance Ltd, Ground Floor, 71 Lower Baggot Street, Dublin D02 P593, Ireland – www.arccompliance.com

For a complete list of Pen & Sword titles please contact
PEN & SWORD BOOKS LTD
47 Church Street, Barnsley, South Yorkshire, S70 2AS, England
E-mail: enquiries@pen-and-sword.co.uk
Website: www.pen-and-sword.co.uk
or
PEN & SWORD BOOKS
1950 Lawrence Road, Havertown, PA 19083, USA
E-mail: uspen-and-sword@casematepublishers.com
Website: www.penandswordbooks.com

Chapter One

German Invasion of Ukraine

During the early morning of 22 June 1941, the German Army launched the largest ground invasion in military history, codenamed Barbarossa – the invasion of the Soviet Union. Both Wehrmacht infantry and panzer divisions bulldozed Germany's massive military arsenal against bewildered Russian forces on every front. The ferocity and effectiveness of the German war machine was so great and swift that some of the Red Army formations, often comprising up to fifteen Russian divisions, were trapped and slowly and systematically annihilated in a hurricane of fire.

For the invasion of Russia, the German Army was distributed into three Army Groups: Army Group North, Army Group Centre and Army Group South; the latter was deployed down the longest stretch of border with Russia. The front reached from central Poland to the Black Sea and was held by six German infantry divisions. The main thrust in the south was directed between the southern edge of the Pripet Marshes and the foothills of the Carpathian Mountains, with the main objective of capturing Ukraine. Over the coming days and weeks, German forces made astonishing progress towards the Dnieper River, despite being continually harassed by strong Russian forces coupled with the Soviet military's scorched-earth policy. By August 1941, the Germans had swung out east of Kyiv (Kiev) and units began mopping up the last remnants in and around the besieged city. When the Battle of Kyiv finally ended on 21 September, almost 665,000 Russian troops had been captured in the encirclement. Exhilarated by the fall of Kyiv, German forces mercilessly pushed forward, leaving a trail of devastation in their wake. Across the whole of the German front in Ukraine, infantry formations hammered deeper into the country, capturing more towns and cities as they advanced.

News of the success of the German invasion of Ukraine was greeted by Hitler with jubilation. In his eyes, the destruction of Ukraine was not just a military objective, it was an ideological goal of eradicating communism and destroying the *Untermenschen*, or subhumans, which included the Ukrainian Jews and ethnic Ukrainians. There were some 40 million people occupying the rich, black earth of Ukraine, which Hitler had decided was to be the new *Lebensraum*, or living space, of the German nation. He was so obsessed with Ukraine that he gave it priority during the invasion of Russia, wanting the territory captured before Moscow, even against the advice of his generals.

The German invasion of Ukraine during the summer of 1941 was swift and decisive, much to the surprise of the generals. However, one of the main reasons that the German attack was so rapid was because there was little resistance. In a number of towns and cities, the Ukrainians actually welcomed the German invaders with flowers or the traditional Ukrainian bread and salt of hospitality and friendship. These German soldiers were surprised that they were welcomed and regarded as liberators from the communist Russian repression of Moscow. In the eyes of many Ukrainians, they had lived under harsh Soviet rule, with Stalin ordering many of their private farms and land to be taken away, including their livestock. What followed in 1933 was almost 7 million Ukrainians dying of starvation in a famine. The repression of the people also included the arrest of thousands of Ukrainians who were regarded as being part of the intelligentsia. Musicians, writers and artists were taken away by the NKVD (People's Commissariat for Internal Affairs), the Soviet secret police. The Ukrainian Orthodox and Catholic Churches were also banned by the Kremlin and only the Russian Orthodox Church was allowed to function.

It is not surprising that the Ukrainian people looked upon the Nazi invasion as liberation from tyranny. However, the people of Ukraine would soon realise they would be replacing one totalitarianism regime for another. Even before the invasion of Ukraine, the Nazis had already planned an extermination policy for the Ukrainian people and would use local collaborators to achieve what they termed a 'Ukrainian statehood' and the formation of a provisional state administration.

Taking rapid control of Ukraine meant that many ordinary German soldiers were instructed to capture the country with whatever means they had at their disposal. On 6 June 1941, in a directive known as the Commissar Order, Hitler outlined that:

> When fighting Bolshevism one can not count on the enemy acting in accordance with the principles of humanity or International Law. In particular it must be expected that the treatment of our prisoners by the political commissars of all types who are the true pillars of resistance will be cruel, inhuman, and dictated by hate . . . Therefore, when captured either in battle or offering resistance, they are to be shot on principle.

Each German soldier had already been taught that the war in the East was one of annihilation, or *Vernichtungskrieg*, the sole purpose of which was the complete destruction of the state, people or an ethnic minority through genocide or the loss of their livelihood. Whether the entire body of ordinary Wehrmacht soldiers believed in a war of annihilation or not is doubtful, but what is evident is that many of them were ordered to march into villages and towns, torch the buildings and murder the inhabitants. Just as serious were the numerous occurrences of surrendered Soviet soldiers and Ukrainian nationalist partisans being shot by regular German soldiers.

In addition to human losses, there was intensive destruction of Ukraine's cultural heritage. Even during the initial advance through Ukraine, the Germans began destroying institutions such as schools, museums, architectural monuments and theatres as well as bookshops and millions of books.

One of the main objectives of the war of annihilation was the destruction of the Jewish population in Ukraine. They were regarded the greatest threat to 'civilization'. In the late 1930s there were about 1.5 million Jews living in the Soviet Republic of Ukraine – the largest Jewish community within the Soviet Union. When Stalin occupied eastern Galicia, western Volhynia, northern Bukovina and southern Bessarabia between 1939 and 1941, the number of Jews in the Ukrainian Soviet Republic rose to 2.45 million. As plans were drawn up to invade Russia, Hitler saw Ukraine as the epicentre of the 'Jew' in the Soviet Union. For this reason, he issued a memorandum entitled 'Guidelines for the Conduct of Troops of Russia', which directly related the Jewish population as a racial group to the broader category of political enemies. This category connected communism to the Jewish race and reinforced the Nazi propagandist notion of a Judeo-Bolshevik crusade designed to try to destroy the German race. For this reason, directives were sent out to all German units instructing them to establish a policy of terror that sanctioned the mass killing of any group deemed a potential threat. What the policy was really instructing was the wholesale destruction of the Ukrainian people, including the entire Jewish population. As a result, what followed in the wake of the German invasion of Ukraine was a holocaust of unparalleled dimension.

Wehrmacht forces during the opening offensive through Ukraine in June 1941. Here, soldiers can be seen marching along a dusty road watched by bewildered Ukrainian civilians. For the invasion of Russia, codenamed Barbarossa, the German Army assembled some 3 million men, divided into a total of 105 infantry divisions and 32 Panzer divisions. Hitler saw Ukraine as a major centre of Soviet industry and mining, which had rich farmland needed for his plans for *Lebensraum*.

German troops capture one of many towns and cities in western Ukraine during the initial phase of operations through the country. German Army Group South was entrusted to drive its powerful forces through Ukraine and advance up to the Volga River, engaging a part of the Red Army in order to clear the way for Army Group North and Army Group Centre to advance on Leningrad and Moscow. However, Hitler gave priority first to the capture of Ukraine, which was against the advice of his generals.

German armoured units, composed of the 1st Panzer Group and the 6th, 17th and 11th Armies supported by Luftflotte 1 and the Romanian 3rd and 4th Armies, enter a Ukrainian city to carry out the capture of the Ukraine Army Group South. Their principal objective was to capture Ukraine and its capital, Kyiv. Among the carnage and decimation are dead horses caught in the fighting.

German armoured vehicles enter a decimated Ukrainian city. Hitler was totally aware that food and agricultural concerns were fundamental to the strategies and tactics of the German Reich. He regarded Ukraine as being ripe for plunder, and it had the space and farmland to provide the economic resources for winning the war. In his eyes, German civilians and soldiers who took over the Ukrainian farms and fields would prevail in Barbarossa, for not only would they be able to feed themselves, but also choke off the Soviet Army's grain supplies.

A German soldier can be seen on a bicycle as a column of horse-drawn supplies pours along a road through a captured Ukrainian town. Ukraine was to be the most important occupied country in the German Reich. The Nazi objective to control Ukraine through *Lebensraum* was not just a romantic desire for a return to the East, but to Hitler, it was a vital strategic component of his imperial and racist vision.

(**Above**) A German halftrack enters a decimated Ukrainian town. The Nazis were determined to capture Ukraine as swiftly and decisively as possible. At the centre of the invasion were plans for *Lebensraum* and the colonisation of the country. By blaming Jews and Bolsheviks for what Hitler termed the 'backwardness' of the region, he demanded the removal of Jews from the territory and their physical destruction. It was for this reason that following in the wake of the Wehrmacht units were Einsatzgruppe death squads that were ordered to roam the countryside and murder Jews and 'Bolsheviks'.

(**Opposite, above**) German supply vehicles in front of the opera house in Kharkov (Kharkiv). On 24 October 1941, Kharkov was captured by Walter von Reichenau's 6th Army. To the Russian Army, Kharkov had been of great strategic importance due to its vital rail and air connections. The city served as a crucial north–south and east–west link between many regions of Ukraine, as well as various areas of the Soviet Union such as Crimea, the Caucasus, the Dnieper region and Donbas. Hitler had outlined to his commanders the importance of capturing the city and its significant military installations. He recognised that the region, especially the Donets Basin, was the foundation of the Russian economy. He believed that control of this vital economic centre would inevitably lead to the collapse of the entire Russian economy. As a result, all military resources were given to the 6th Army to capture the Kharkov industrial area and the city itself.

(**Opposite, below**) A column of horse-drawn transport can be seen advancing along a dirt track on the approaches of a Ukrainian city.

German troops pictured next to a destroyed Russian tank during their march through the western regions of Ukraine.

Dusty, dirty and dishevelled German troops on the march across the vast open expanse of Ukraine. Many soldiers were unaware of the extent of the country and often lacked proper provisions to sustain themselves for any appreciable length of time. In spite of these problems, the advance was rapid and overwhelming.

Almost as soon as a town or city was captured, the Germans immediately set up various road blocks and control points in preparation for governmental control of the area. In this photograph, engineers are preparing a security control point on a road.

(**Above**) A **flak** gun unit has temporarily halted during its advance through Ukraine. Many units had advanced so quickly they often outstripped their vital supply lines and it was necessary to stop in order for them to catch up to the leading columns.

(**Opposite, above**) German halftracks supported by supply wagons towed by animal draught are on the move in a decimated Ukrainian city.

(**Opposite, below**) Police and Wehrmacht officers tour the rear areas of conquered Ukraine territory in the summer of 1941. When an area had been captured, German authorities immediately set up regional offices that would be controlled under civil administration. These offices were often governed by a German or Ukrainian 'Party Chief'. In very important areas, or where a German Army detachment remained, the local administration was always led by a German. In areas where it was deemed less important, local personnel were in charge. These offices were also charged with recruiting volunteers into local military controlled areas. They also promoted local Ukrainian nationalist organisations, which would support the Wehrmacht and the Einsatzgruppen. It was considered very important to have cohesion among the army, death squads and local collaborators so that they could work together in removing Jews and 'Bolsheviks' from their districts.

A series of photographs showing captured Russian soldiers. The Nazis had complete disregard for the laws and customs of war. As a result, during the Wehrmacht's march through Ukraine they indiscriminately executed captured commissars and starved to death ordinary Soviet soldiers. Orders had been sent out to the chain of command prior to the invasion that all Soviet Jews and political commissars, and some officers, communists, intellectuals and female combatants were to be systematically targeted for execution. Soldiers were shot if they surrendered, were injured or ill, or were unable to keep up with forced marches. Supporting the Wehrmacht were a growing number of Ukrainian Auxiliary units. Collaborators were an essential component to the Nazis as they needed as many people as possible in the field as willing accomplices to murder prisoners, Jews and 'Bolsheviks'.

A Hitler propaganda poster that says, in Ukrainian, 'Hitler the Liberator'.

German soldiers smile with their sign that reads, *'Hier beginnt der Arsch der Welt!'*, which translates as, 'Here begins the ass of the world!'

Donned with flowers, German soldiers smile with local Ukrainian peasants. Across a number of regions, the Ukrainians welcomed the German invaders with flowers or the traditional Ukrainian bread and salt of hospitality and friendship.

A German motorcyclist seems unperturbed by the local villagers as he has left his bolt-action rifle against his motorcycle. Across parts of the country, there had been a widespread belief that Nazi Germany, as the declared enemy of Poland and the Soviet Union, was the Ukrainians' natural ally for their independence. However, this belief was quickly crushed. By the end of June 1941, the Nazis set up a Ukrainian statehood and formation of a provisional state administration, all aimed at destroying Ukrainian culture and implementing racial policies that included the mass killing of Jews.

The first of three photographs showing captured Russian soldiers in Ukraine. Anti-Bolshevism, anti-Semitism and racism are often cited as the main reasons behind the mass death of Soviet prisoners. The Wehrmacht's advance had been so rapid through Ukraine that German planners had not prepared for housing or feeding prisoners. It is estimated that in 1941, three to four Soviet soldiers were captured for each one killed.

Two photographs showing bread being handed out to prisoners in the camp at Vinnytsia in July 1941.

A German halftrack advances through a captured town. An officer salutes to the passing vehicle while the locals look on.

A series of images showing Russian prisoners captured during the German invasion of Ukraine. Although these soldiers have not been indiscriminately executed, many were escorted away to a collection point where they would then be sent on to transit camps where they were kept under terrible conditions and often starved to death. Those who managed to survive were then transported to various labour or concentration camps in Europe, where they would be worked to death.

The price of surrendering to German forces in Ukraine. In some regions of Ukraine, German soldiers often refused to take prisoners and shot soldiers who tried to surrender. Thousands were executed on the spot as partisans. The second photograph shows a trench full of Russian captives that have been murdered.

As battles intensified in some regions of Ukraine, both Soviet forces and the local population withdrew further east. In this photograph, soldiers and civilians withdraw through a town that has come under heavy attack.

(**Above**) Ukrainian civilians are seen selling their wares on a pavement following the German occupation of their town in the summer of 1941.

(**Opposite, above**) Ukrainian women peel potatoes for German troops during a pause in military operations. Often, German troops arrived in conquered towns and villages giving the impression they were liberators against Soviet 'tyranny'. In return, the locals were frequently helpful to the German military in preparing food, cooking and even washing uniforms. Many had no idea of the brutal regime that was beginning to grip the country or what the Jewish people were being subjected to behind the advancing troops.

(**Opposite, below**) Touring the city of Kyiv is Alfred Rosenberg (centre) and Erich Koch (right). Rosenberg was the Nazi Party's chief racial theorist and oversaw Hitler's racial and ethnic policies. In July 1941, he was appointed head of the Reich Ministry for the Occupied Eastern Territories (Reichsministerium für die besetzten Ostgebiete). It was Rosenberg that presented to his *Führer* his plan for the organisation of the conquered Eastern territories, suggesting the establishment of new administrative districts. Ukraine would be one of the main Eastern districts of the Reichskommissariat Ostland (Reich Commissariat of Eastland). As for Erich Koch, he was appointed the Reichskommissar in the Reichskommissariat Ukraine from September 1941. He had control of the Gestapo and uniformed police. His first act as Reichskommissar was to close local schools, declaring that Ukrainian children did not need schools. Koch was a brutal and unpleasant individual and once said, 'If I meet a Ukrainian worthy of being seated at my table, I must have him shot.'

Chapter Two

Security Policy of Terror

As German forces marched through Ukraine, more sinister activities were already generating fear and terror in the rear areas of the country. Advancing simultaneously with the Wehrmacht were special Einsatzgruppen (deployment forces or task forces), which were special SS (Schutzstaffel) paramilitary death squads responsible for mass murder on a mammoth scale. Under the direction of Reichsführer-SS Heinrich Himmler and led by the notorious Otto Ohlendorf, these special forces were put together from the Security Police (Sicherheitspolizei) and Security Service (Sicherheitsdienst) as well as parts of the SS. Together they would responsible for the security policy directive, which would include massacres on an unprecedented scale against partisans, civilians, gypsies, Jews and intelligentsia, including members of the priesthood and anyone else they deemed hostile elements to 'German civilization'. These special murder squads had initially operated in territories occupied by the Wehrmacht during the German invasion of Poland in 1939 and their operations were regarded as a great success. Now in Ukraine, they would work hand in hand with the Order Police battalions (Ordnungspolizei), various security police units, foreign auxiliary personnel, Waffen-SS and even regular German soldiers. Pitiless and callously thoughtless to human suffering, they were entrusted to suppress the inhabitants of Ukraine. To them, genocidal actions were the most effective instrument available to destroy all elements hostile to the banner of Nazism. Ukraine would be a blooding on an unprecedented scale.

When the German Army launched its invasion of Ukraine in the summer of 1941, Soviet forces struggled to hold their forces together as retreating troops were being attacked on a broad front by constant air and ground attacks. Yet, the Red Army's withdrawal had not degenerated into mass panic. Many units saw the Germans as their liberators from Soviet tyranny and surrendered, often without a fight. In the face of these wholesale surrenders, the Nazis were nevertheless not going to be influenced by a nation they regarded as subhuman. In order to accomplish their *Führer*'s policy of terror, the Einsatzgruppen were given the primary task of efficiently and methodically annihilating all actual and potential sources of Ukrainian leadership and resistance. This task would be carried out with lethal effect using these new paramilitary death squads following in the wake of the advancing German Army.

To deal with the enemies in the Soviet Union there were four Einsatzgruppe task forces, each numbering 500–990 men. The task forces were divided into units A, B, C and D and were under the operational control of the higher SS police chiefs in their zones of operation. The first three groups were attached respectively to Army Group North, Centre and South, whilst D was assigned to activities through Latvia and Lithuania. Einsatzgruppe C was given operational duties in the south of Ukraine. As soon as these special forces entered the country, they quickly engaged in humiliation and murder. These took the form of shootings and hangings in the towns and villages such as Lviv, Lutsk, Rovno (Rivne), Zhytomyr, Pereyaslav (Pereiaslav), Yagotyn (Yahotyn), Lubny, Kyiv, Rostov, Tarnopol (Ternopil) and Kharkov. In an operational report to Berlin, Einsatzgruppe C reported that, on 5 July 1941:

> 15 Jews were executed as reprisals for the bestial murder of the Ukrainian nationalist leader Dr Kirnychy in Rudki [Rudky]. The Ukrainian population on their part set the synagogue and Jewish houses on fire. 150 Ukrainians were found murdered in Stryj [Stryi]. In the course of the search, it was possible to arrest 12 Communists who were responsible for the murder of the Ukrainians. It concerns 11 Jews and 1 Ukrainian who were shot with the participation of the entire population of Stryj.

What followed through July 1941 was unrestrained terror against the local population and captured soldiers. All of the killings were regarded as justified reprisals for alleged violence perpetrated by retreating Soviet soldiers. This included the shooting of approximately eighty Jewish men in Dobromil (Dobromyl) on 30 June 1941 as an act of reprisal. Einsatzgruppe C command said they were in Ukraine in order to protect the German race and its allies, and the killing of the Jews was in order to protect the Germanisation of Ukraine. During July, Einsatzgruppe C murdered some 7,000 Jews in what it called 'retaliation for the inhuman atrocities' committed by the Jews in Zviahel. The mass execution of Jewish men continued with unabated ferocity. Einsatzgruppe C reported:

> 40 men were liquidated on the basis of well-founded denunciations made by inhabitants. Mainly Jews between 20 and 40 years of age were rounded up ... apart from these executions in Lvov [Lviv], reprisal measures were carried out at the other places also: 132 Jews, for instance, were shot in Dobromil.

Einsatzgruppe C, which had begun it killings across western Ukraine to Kharkov and Rostov-on-Don, reported they massacred about 3,000 Jews in what was known as the Lviv pogroms. It reported that the cities and towns of Tarnopol, Zolochiv, Kremenets, Kharkov, Zhytomyr and Kyiv were also targeted, and thousands were murdered. But it was not just the murder squads that were involved in numerous killings; the Wehrmacht were also responsible. In August 1941, General Walther von Reichenau, commander of the 6th Army, ordered his men to support Einsatzgruppe units including Ukrainian Auxiliary units in the rounding up and murdering of Jews of Bila Tserkva. Troops marched into the town and killed the entire adult population and left behind ninety Jewish children who had been dumped in an abandoned building. They were crying and hungry.

SS-Obersturmführer August Häfner of Sonderkommando 4a saw the following murders on 21 August 1941 and later testified what he had witnessed:

> I went to the woods alone. The Wehrmacht had already dug a grave. The children were brought along in a tractor. I had nothing to do with this technical procedure. The Ukrainians were standing around trembling. The children were taken down from the tractor. They were lined up along the top of the grave and shot so that they fell into it. The Ukrainians did not aim at any particular part of the body. They fell into the grave. The wailing was indescribable. I shall never forget the scene throughout my life. I find it very hard to bear. I particularly remember a small fair-haired girl who took me by the hand. She too was shot later ... The grave was near some woods. It was not near the rifle range. The execution must have taken place in the afternoon at about 3:30 or 4:00. It took place the day after the discussions at the Feldkommandanten ... Many children were hit four or five times before they died.

This report was one of many of hundreds describing countless shootings and executions carried out by the Einsatzgruppen, SS police battalions, the Wehrmacht, and local Ukrainian collaborators. During the summer of 1941, thousands of Jewish men and boys of military age throughout Ukraine were being systematically rounded up and hanged in public places or murdered in mass shootings. In Crimea, the Einsatzgruppen conducted extensive killings in northern Transylvania, Chernivtsi, Kishinev, and across the whole Crimea region including the Crimean Peninsula. Of their own accord, the German Army and the Waffen-SS offered assistance in the rounding up and killing of civilians and Jews. Military progress through Ukraine was swift and bloody. The thoroughness and brutality with which these 'cleansing actions' were conducted was violent and ruthless. It was not just men who were targeted by the special action forces in Ukraine. Einsatzgruppe C and SS brigades under the command of Friedrich Jeckeln began ordering the shooting of entire Jewish communities in the western city of Kamianets-Podilskyi at the end of August. According to task force records, between 26 and 28 August, they shot 23,600 Jewish men, women and children into an enormous pit on the outskirts of the city.

A few days following the Kamianets-Podilskyi massacre, on 5 September, an Einsatzgruppe unit drove into a shtetl, a small town with a predominantly Jewish population. The commander of Einsatzgruppe C, Brigadeführer Otto Rasch, then ordered the extermination of any Jews found. During the course of a few hours, they rounded up 1,500 Jews and took them to the Jewish cemetery, located on the outskirts of Pavoloch. The frightened and bewildered Jews were ordered to dig a mass grave. They were made to kneel next to the grave and were shot. The pit full of dead bodies was filled in to conceal the evidence of the slaughter.

In other areas of operations, the Einsatzgruppen continued to report on their success. Following the capture of Kyiv, which had taken several weeks more than was scheduled, Einsatzgruppe C marched into the city. Here, the task force units were surprised to be greeted warmly by the Ukrainian citizens, who believed the Germans would free them from Soviet rule and atrocities. However, these soldiers had been given specific duties to carry out cleansing actions exclusively against the Jewish community. Within hours of their arrival, the soldiers had looted homes and businesses, and also detained a number of Jews. Due to the difficulties of collecting so many Jews from the area, copies of a poster were plastered all around the city and surrounding villages outlining that they needed to prepare for resettlement. It read:

> Kikes [a contemptuous term for a Jewish person] of the city of Kiev [Kyiv] and vicinity! On Monday, 29 September, you are to appear by 7:00 a.m. with your possessions, money, documents, valuables and warm clothing at Dorogozhitshaya Street, next to the Jewish cemetery. Failure to appear is punishable by death

Once the Jews had congregated that morning, they were marched to Babi Yar, a ravine only 2 miles from the city centre. Troops from Einsatzgruppe C, Sonderkommando 4a, 92 Police Regiment South and Ukrainian Auxiliary units escorted them. A truck driver at the scene described what he saw:

> I watched what happened when the Jews – men, women and children – arrived. The Ukrainians led them past a number of different places where one after another they had to remove their luggage, then their coats, shoes, and over garments and also underwear. They had to leave their valuables in a designated place. There was a special pile for each article of clothing. It all happened very quickly ... I don't think it was even a minute from the time each Jew took off his coat before he was standing there completely naked ...
>
> Once undressed, the Jews were led into the ravine which was about 150 meters long and 30 meters wide and a good 15 meters deep. ... When they reached the bottom of the ravine they were seized by members of the Schultpolizei [Schutzpolizei] and made to lie down on top of Jews who had already been shot. That all happened very quickly. The corpses were literally in layers. A police marksman came along and shot each Jew in the neck with a submachine gun. ... I saw these marksman [*sic*] stand on layers of corpses and shoot one after the other. ... The marksman would walk across the bodies of the executed Jews to the next Jew who had meanwhile lain down and shoot him.

Sonderkommando 4a soldier Kurt Werner testified later about the killing process:

> The Jews had to lie face down on the earth by the ravine walls. There were three groups of marksmen down at the bottom of the ravine, each made up of about twelve men. Groups of Jews were sent down to each of these execution squads simultaneously. Each successive group of Jews had to lie down on top of the bodies of those that had already been shot. The marksmen stood behind the Jews and killed them with a shot in the neck. I still

> recall today the complete terror of the Jews when they first caught sight of the bodies as they reached the top edge of the ravine. Many Jews cried out in terror. It's almost impossible to imagine what nerves of steel it took to carry out that dirty work down there. It was horrible ... I had to spend the whole morning down in the ravine. For some of the time I had to shoot continuously.

The Babi Yar massacre lasted from 29 to 30 September. Within twenty-four hours, Einsatzgruppe C, Sonderkommando 4a and their police reinforcements murdered 33,771 Jewish men, women and children, burying them crudely in the ravine. A survivor named Elena Efimovna Borodyanskaya-Knysh had been brought to Babi Yar with her young daughter on 29 September. She testified later:

> When my little girl saw all this, she started to cry ... She was four at the time. Everyone had been stripped naked ... Around midnight, in German, came the command for us to line up along the edge of the ravine. I didn't wait for the next command but immediately tossed my little girl into the pit and then fell in after her. A second later, bodies started falling on top of me. Then it grew quiet. About fifteen minutes went by, and then they brought in another party. Again a shout rang out; again the bloody bodies and dying people began to fall into the pit. I could feel that my daughter wasn't moving. I leaned up against her, covered her with my body, and squeezing my hands into fists, placed them under her chin, so my little girl wouldn't suffocate. My daughter started to move. I tried to raise myself up, so as not to crush her. There was so much blood all around us. The shooting had been going on since nine o'clock that morning. Bodies were lying on top of me and beneath me.

In its situation report to Berlin on 2 October 1941, Einsatzgruppe C wrote:

> Sonderkommando 4a in collaboration with Einsatzgruppe [headquarters] and two Kommandos of Police Regiment South, executed 33,771 Jews in Kyiv on 29 September and 30, 1941.

Over the following months, Babi Yar remained in use as an execution site for gypsies and Soviet prisoners of war. It is estimated that 100,000 Ukrainians were shot into the grave in Babi Yar, making it one of the largest mass graves in the world. Similar executions were undertaken across other areas of Ukraine. By the end of October 1941 alone, Jeckeln's SS and Einsatzgruppe units had murdered more than 100,000 Jewish men, women and children. The Einsatzgruppe forces in Ukraine noted that within just nine months, its force had killed more than 90,000 people. It boastfully averaged 340 persons per day, comprising mainly Jews, gypsies, Asiatics, and what it called 'undesirables'. Between 16 November and 15 December 1941, it averaged killing 700 people each day. The intensity of these cleansing actions was stated in a report of April 1942:

> The Crimea is freed of Jews. Only occasionally some small groups are turning up, especially in the northern areas. In cases where single Jews could

camouflage themselves by means of forged papers, etc., they will, nevertheless, be recognised sooner or later, as experience has taught.

Supporting the Einsatzgruppen during their intensive barbaric operations in 1941 were the Order Police. They conducted a number of brutal massacres and were involved in the mass killings at Babi Yar and Stanisławów. Police Battalion 303 was one of six that operated in Ukraine during the initial stages of the invasion of the Soviet Union. It was not only engaged in mopping up Soviet pockets of resistance, but also undertook security actions against the local population, which included hanging partisans and razing farmsteads to the ground. It was also involved in the massacre at Chudniv in early September 1941, killing hundreds of Jews, and it operated alongside Einsatzkommando squads, where it was involved in killing actions in and around Zhytomyr. Police Battalion 303, along with the Einsatzgruppen, undertook a number of actions in the rear areas, targeting the Jewish population. Police Battalion 303 also assisted the Einsatzgruppen at Babi Yar. Murders did not end at Babi Yar; Police Battalion 303 went on to hunt down partisans and Soviet army stragglers. Their killing spree was only reduced by the onset of winter in the rear of Army Group South. A number of policemen were actually decorated for their 'pacification activities' and awarded with medals for their 'valour'.

Also operating in Ukraine was Police Battalion 319. Although its cleansing actions were undertaken on a comparatively smaller scale than those of Police Battalion 318, its operations in the heartlands of the country were deemed effective and pacification successful.

One police unit, however, that was responsible for the murders of about 45,000 people, was Police Battalion 320. It crossed over the Soviet border in the middle of August 1941 and its advance eastwards led it to the towns and cities of Przemyśl, Lviv and Tarnopol. Its mission was for 'special employment' and from the moment it was employed, the battalion would be regularly involved in genocide actions against the Jewish communities. The police units undertook a series of widespread massacres in Starokostiantyniv, Kamianets-Podilskyi, Minkovtsy, Zwianczyk and Sokolek. Those that managed to escape the slaughters were hunted down and killed. The police battalion was later given anti-partisan duties in February 1942 and then transferred south along the Mius River, in the area of Taganrog at the rear of the 1st Panzer Army.

Order Police relax while billeted in a Ukrainian town during an operation in 1941. The police played a vital role in the execution of the Holocaust in Ukraine and supported extensively widespread executions of Jewish communities.

Order Police officers pose for the camera during operations in Ukraine in 1941. There were six police battalions operating in Ukraine during the initial stages of the invasion of the Soviet Union. They were not only engaged in mopping up Soviet pockets of resistance, but also undertook security actions against the local population, which included hanging partisans and razing farmsteads to the ground.

Police officers touring the rear areas during operations in Ukraine in 1941. The police battalions were subordinated to the SS and not under the command of the German Army. Their primary role in Ukraine was deployment in areas of German-occupied Europe while operating in the rear areas of the Wehrmacht, Waffen-SS and Einsatzgruppen in Russia.

The first of two photographs showing police and Wehrmacht officers at a garrison in Ukraine during the summer of 1941. Police battalions operated alongside the Einsatzgruppen and were ordered to sweep across large areas of the country, roaming and searching as they advanced, killing as many members of Jewish communities as possible. Assisting these massacres, the Order Police also had the help of local Ukrainian police units and auxiliaries. Many of the killings, especially in Ukraine, were undertaken by fellow Ukrainians commanded by German officers.

Also assisting the Order Police were local police units and auxiliaries, pictured here.

A photograph showing the 115th Battalion of Ukrainian 'Schuma' (Schutzmannschaft) in 1943. These policemen were part of the Ukrainian Auxiliary Police or Ukrainische Hilfspolizei, which was the official title of the local police formation set up by the German administration in eastern Galicia and Reichskommissariat Ukraine.

During what was called the *Intelligenzaktion* (intelligentsia action), a Ukrainian man suspected of being a member of the intelligentsia is being led away by an Order Police officer. Behind the officer appear to be Einsatzgruppe members. Numerous police battalions were sent to Ukraine under the disguise of 'police duties' or as army reinforcements. It did not take long before many units became involved in various brutal and heinous actions where they carried out shootings of Jews and members of the intelligentsia. *(Yad Vashem)*

The first of four disturbing photographs showing the public hangings following in an *Intelligenzaktion*. These actions were primarily aimed at teachers, priests, physicians and other prominent members of Ukrainian society, and were first seen in the heartlands of Poland in 1939. Hitler had ordered the execution of the intelligentsia and the social elites to stop them from organising the Polish nation against the Nazis, and prevent the occupation and colonisation of the country. In 1941, he wanted to replicate the same action in Ukraine to avoid a possible uprising. (*Yad Vashem*)

(**Below**) The first of three photographs showing Ukrainian men being led to the gallows during a public hanging. Attached to the front of their coats are signs informing the local inhabitants of why they have been sentenced to death. The victims have been paraded through the streets in order to visibly degrade them and act as a stark warning of punishment by death. Local Ukrainian collaborators wearing white armbands have erected the makeshift gallows and are using empty oil drums for the convicted men to stand on. Behind the collaborators are members of the Einsatzgruppen. *(Yad Vashem)*

A photograph taken during the Lviv pogrom. A blood-soaked and frightened Jewish woman is evidently being chased by men and children through the city. The massacres were perpetrated by Ukrainian nationalists and Einsatzgruppe units from 30 June to 2 July, and from 25 to 29 July 1941. Following the capture of the city, a full pogrom of the area was ordered, with Jews being taken from their homes and forced to clean the streets on their hands and knees. Jewish women were also attacked, stripped naked and beaten, with local Ukrainian residents implicated in some of the attacks.

A photograph taken by a Wehrmacht propaganda unit showing Ukrainians attacking a Jewish gentleman during the Lviv pogrom in July 1941. It is estimated that some 2,000 Jews disappeared or were murdered by the Einsatzgruppen. Later that year, the Lviv Ghetto was established, which at its peak held about 120,000 Jews.

Two photographs taken in sequence, showing the arrest of local Ukrainians by Order Police. The mission of the Order Police throughout Ukraine would be to kill members of the Ukrainian leadership and assist in the executions of members of the Jewish communities. *(Yad Vashem)*

Russian prisoners have been collected and await transportation to a camp inside a Ukrainian town. Their fate can only be imagined. *(Yad Vashem)*

Reichsführer-SS Heinrich Himmler accepts the well wishes of SS police officers on the occasion of his birthday at SS headquarters in the Hegewald bei Zhytomyr compound.

The Order Police have murdered a group of Ukrainian men during a local cleansing action. During the German occupation of western Ukraine, the Jews were terrorised, deprived of all means of survival, and totally isolated from any type of help or assistance. This made it easier for the German occupation authorities, especially during the first wave of killings in June and July 1941. *(Yad Vashem)*

It is unclear what the local inhabitants are doing in this photograph. It appears that members of the Order Police have set the men to work in a field. More sinister is that they could be digging their own graves, but this is pure speculation. *(Yad Vashem)*

Two photographs taken in sequence, showing Jewish deportees under German guard being force-marched through the streets of Kamianets to an execution site outside of the city. These Jews had been deported to Kamianets – a city in western Ukraine that was occupied by German forces in late June 1941. The deportees comprised mainly Polish and Russian Jews, but there were numerous refugees from Western Europe. Einsatzgruppen, Hungarian soldiers and the Ukrainian Auxiliary Police (Ukrainische Hilfspolizei) had been given specific orders to march the Jews out of the city and murder them, which would be known as the Kamianets-Podilskyi massacre.

Soviet soldiers together with local inhabitants are escorted through the town by a German soldier.

Jews at the killing site outside of Kamianets-Podilskyi. The victims have just arrived, as they have not been ordered to undress. They are all minutes away from being killed. In the summer of 1941, thousands of foreign and undocumented Jews living in the eastern Carpathians were targeted for expulsion by the Hungarian National Central Alien Control Office. In July and August, approximately 20,000 of these Jews were rounded up by Hungarian units and deported over the Ukrainian border into the waiting hands of the SS. After being transported to Kolomyia, these Jews were marched to Kamianets-Podilskyi. Not knowing what to do with the influx of Jews, on 27 August, SS units, military police, Ukrainian Auxiliary units and Hungarian troops gathered in Kamianets-Podilskyi. They collected the Jewish deportees, along with local Jews, and marched them 10 miles outside of the city.

Two disturbing photographs showing Jews from Kamianets-Podilskyi awaiting their fate before being taken to the murder site. They would be marched to their place of execution, ordered to undress and then shot into a large, freshly dug pit.

A widely seen, distressing image of a Jewish man about to be shot on the edge of a pit by a member of the Einsatzgruppen, probably on 28 July 1941, in Berdychiv. It is estimated that 20,000 to 30,000 Jews were murdered in Berdychiv.

Naked victims shot into a pit following the Kamianets-Podilskyi massacre. According to Einsatzgruppe records, they shot 23,600 Jewish men, women and children into an enormous pit on the outskirts of the city between 26 and 28 August.

Order Police have rounded up Soviet stragglers that were found roaming the Ukrainian countryside.

Order Police and Ukrainian Auxiliary Police humiliate a Jewish man by cutting his sidelocks. Such acts of abuse were common in Eastern Europe and the humiliation was a form of punishment, often for supposed 'racial defilement'. *(Yad Vashem)*

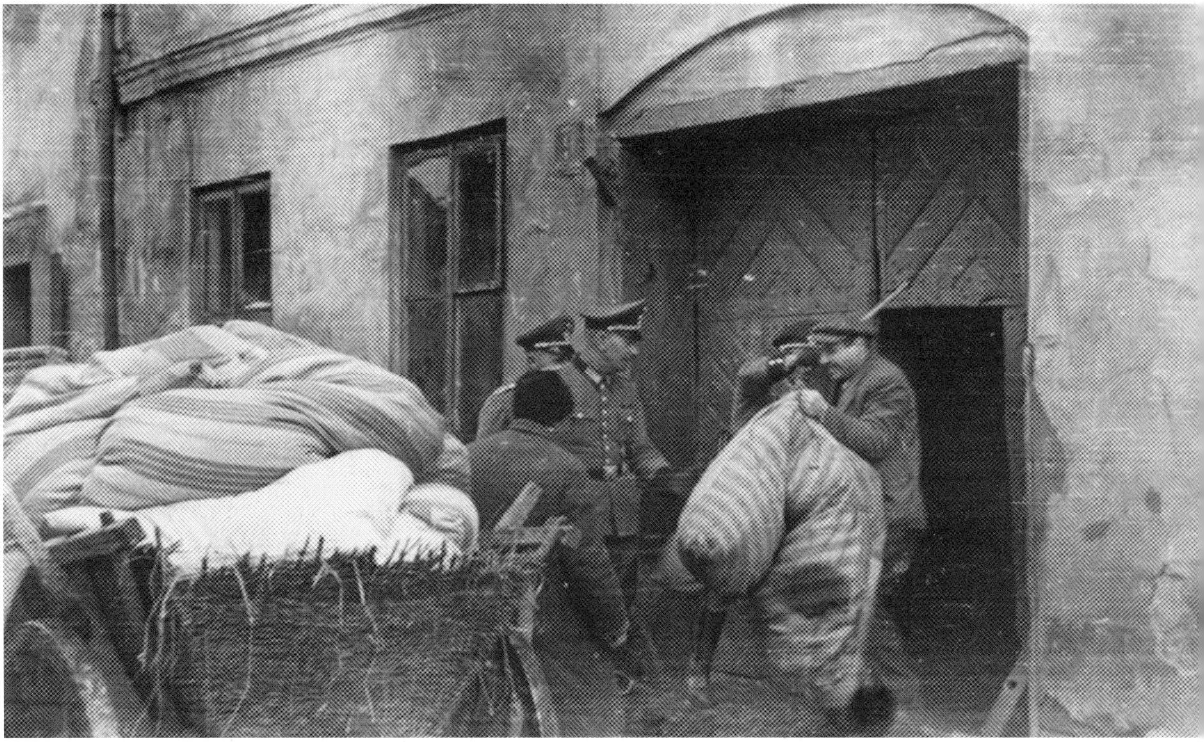

Order Police have been tasked with the removal of Jewish people from their homes during a cleansing action. As soon as the German Army captured a region there was a period of more or less unrestrained terror. This included a series of operations comprising numerous police battalions assisting the Einsatzgruppen in a series of widespread cleansing actions across the country. *(Yad Vashem)*

Order Police stand next to a vehicle prior to a cleansing action. The Order Police soon became an integral part of the persecution of the Jews in Ukraine and joined other German occupation forces in trying to eradicate their very existence. *(Yad Vashem)*

Order Police officers pose for the camera armed with stick grenades. These grenades were often used to flush out people hiding in holes or undergrowth, where they could not be easily captured.

An Einsatzgruppe member leads blindfolded Jews to an execution area. This was a typical Einsatzgruppe execution. Until July and August 1941, German discrimination and persecution of Ukrainian Jews had been restricted to only those living in the Nazi-occupied region of western Ukraine.

A Ukrainian Police officer with a wide armband instructs Jews to move along a street during the pogrom in Sambir.

Einsatzgruppe soldiers can be seen shooting Jews who are in a ditch. Here, troops armed with rifles point their weapons at innocent civilians, while they stand with their backs to the firing squad. Thousands of people in Ukraine were murdered in this way in 1941, and it was often standard practice to kill them in large pits so their bodies could be quickly be covered and traces of their murders concealed from the world.

The first two of four photographs taken in sequence at Babi Yar showing preparation works for digging a huge pit to bury thousands of murdered Jews. The first image shows an SS guard speaking with local Ukrainian women while Soviet prisoners carry out forced labour. These images were taken by a German propaganda unit photographer.

A photograph taken by the German Air Force in September 1943, showing an aerial view of the Babi Yar ravine. *(NARA)*

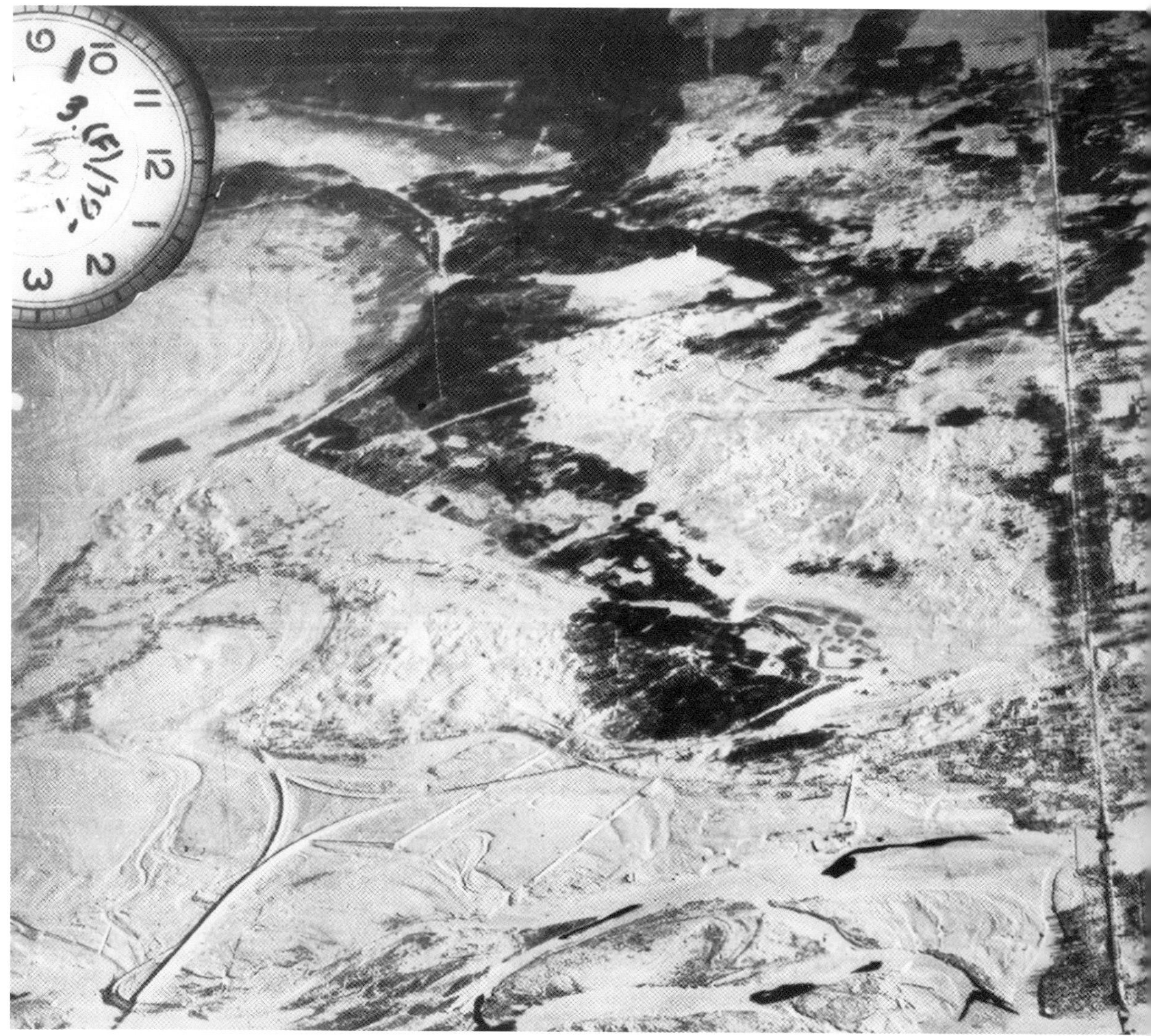

(**Above**) Another photograph taken by the German Air Force in September 1943, showing an aerial view of the Babi Yar ravine. *(NARA)*

(**Opposite**) Two photographs taken in sequence, showing SS officers searching through massive piles of clothing belonging to the more than 33,000 Jews murdered at the nearby Babi Yar killing site. The SS forced the victims to undress and leave their belongings behind before they were massacred. A few weeks after the massacre at Babi Yar, the Romanian army and police committed an almost similar crime, killing around 25,000 Jews in Odesa on 23–24 October. Most of the remaining Jews there were driven to northern Transnistria, into the ethnic German settlement areas around Berezivka, where they were subsequently murdered by the ethnic German Selbstschutz – an SS 'self-protection' organisation. Around Christmas 1941, the Romanian authorities massacred the inmates of the so-called Golta camps Akhmetchetka, Bohdanivka, and Domanivka, in which tens of thousands of Jews from other regions had been held. The majority of the camps' inmates had been killed by March 1942. Only in August 1942 did the Romanian government decide they no longer wanted to actively participate in the Holocaust.

An unidentified Einsatzgruppe unit executes civilians kneeling by the side of a mass grave. During the summer months of 1941, SS and police bases were established in occupied areas of the Soviet Union, and the southern part of this organisation was known as Russia-South. Under its command was Einsatzgruppe C, which was operating in western and later in northern Ukraine, and Einsatzgruppe D, which was in charge of the mass killings in southern Ukraine. By the autumn of 1941, Einsatzgruppe C was directed by the chief of the German security police in Kiev. *(NARA)*

A Jewish man has been shot by a German police unit while being deported in October 1941. He obviously was ill or too weak to keep up with those being force-marched. A young boy looks on as he passes on a road. During the Einsatzgruppe advance eastwards, they left behind regular German police units, notably the Ukraine Police Regiment South (Police Battalions 45, 303 and 314) and Police Battalions 304, 315 and 320.

On 16 October 1941, Ukrainian Jews from Lubny were ordered by the authorities to take their belongings and make their way to an assembly point in a field just outside of the town. Unknown to these people, the Einsatzgruppen were preparing to murder them all. *(Yad Vashem)*

A photograph of the Lubny Jews in a collection area before being escorted from the town and murdered. All of their belongings have been gathered in piles. On 16 October, at a site outside the city, 4,500 Jews from the area were murdered. *(Yad Vashem)*

Over 1,000 Jews from Lubny are ordered to assemble in an open field for 'resettlement' before being massacred by the Einsatzgruppen. *(Yad Vashem)*

A series of photographs taken in sequence, showing men women and children awaiting execution outside the town of Lubny. Einsatzgruppe detachments forced these Ukrainian Jews to undress before they were massacred. These photos were part of a series taken by a German military photographer. Copies from this collection were later used as evidence in war crimes trials. *(Yad Vashem)*

This tragic photograph shows a local police unit assisting Einsatzgruppe operations during a cleansing action in the rear areas. A peasant mother and her child are executed at the side of a pit outside the village of Myropil, Zhytomyr General District, on 13 October 1941.

A Ukrainian Jewish man has been murdered in northern Ukraine during a forced march and lies in the snow, sometime in late 1941. During this period, the first SS brigade of the Waffen-SS committed mass murders in northern Ukraine.

Chapter Three

Change of Policy

Regardless of having achieved the execution of many of the Jewish community across Ukraine, including what the Nazis deemed hostile elements of the Reich, commanders in the field soon realised that their methods of mass murder had many disadvantages. Firstly, the killings were difficult to conceal and were often witnessed by large numbers of persons who were unauthorised to do so, including members of the Wehrmacht, who frequently complained about the brutality. This was not so much out of sympathy for those being executed, but for the psychological effects it had on their men. Himmler made it clear to the Wehrmacht that they would have to simply accept the wholesale liquidation of Jews in Ukraine as policy and cooperate. However, he was aware that they needed a better technique for murdering large numbers of people very quickly and as anonymously as possible. One idea of Himmler's was killing in gas vans. Gas had been used by the T4 Euthanasia Programme in Germany to kill the insane and incurably ill. The method was a complete success and ran for two years, but due to growing public opinion against euthanasia in Germany, the killings were reluctantly suspended. Now it was proposed that this system of killing should be used outside Germany against enemies of the state, especially those from the East. The invasion of the Soviet Union in the summer of 1941 gave access to thousands of Jews and other creeds regarded by the Nazis as 'subhuman', and plans were immediately set in motion to kill as many as possible using gas.

Over the coming weeks, while the Wehrmacht continued to advance ever deeper into Russia, gas was introduced for the first time to the Einsatzgruppen. A special airtight vehicle had been built to resemble an ambulance or refrigerator truck. Although many thousands of Jews and Soviets were captured and herded into the new gas vans and murdered, these vehicles were not very popular amongst the perpetrators since operating them was deemed more unpleasant than achieving mass executions by shooting. Nevertheless, the gas vans were to remain the preferred method of liquidating Jews in Russia and Ukraine, and were intended to lighten the task of carrying out killing operations in the occupied territories. In May 1942, a report was sent to SS-Obersturmbannführer Walter Rauff, who played a key role in the murdering of Jews in gas vans.

Field Post Office No. 32704
B. Nr 40/42

Reich Secret Document

To: SS-Obersturmbannführer Rauff
Berlin

The overhauling of the vans of [Einsatz]Gruppen D and C has been completed ...

I have had the vans of [Einsatz]Gruppe D disguised as house-trailers, by having a single window shutter fixed to each side of the small vans, and on the large ones, two shutters, such as one often sees on farmhouses in the country. The vans had become so well known that not only the authorities but the civilian population referred to them as the 'Death Vans' as soon as one appeared. In my opinion the vans cannot be kept secret for any length of time even if they are camouflaged.

The brakes of the gas van which I took from Taganrog to Simferopol were damaged on the way ... When I reached Stalino [Donetsk] and Gorlovka a few days later the drivers of the vans there complained of the same trouble ...

I also gave instructions that all personnel should stay as far away as possible from the vans when the gassing is in progress to prevent damage to their health in the event of gas leaking out. I would like to take this opportunity to call attention to the following: several of the special units let their own men do the unloading after gassing.

I pointed out to the commanders of the Sonderkommando [special unit] concerned the enormous psychological and physical harm this may cause the men, possibly later even if not immediately. The men complained to me of headaches that recur after each such unloading. Nevertheless there is reluctance to change the orders because it is feared that if prisoners are used for this work they might make use of a favourable moment to escape. I request appropriate instructions in order to save the men from suffering harm.

The gassing is generally not carried out correctly. In order to get the *Aktion* finished as quickly as possible the driver presses down on the accelerator as far as it will go. As a result the persons to be executed die of suffocation and do not doze off as was planned. It has proved that if my instructions are followed and the levers are properly adjusted death comes faster and the prisoners fall asleep peacefully. Distorted faces and excretions, such as were observed before, no longer occur.

Today I shall continue my journey to [Einsatz]Gruppe B, where I may be reached for further instructions.

By early 1942, government policy towards the Jews began to change. Following the Wannsee Conference, it was agreed that the Jews would be eradicated, but there would be more structured procedures put in place. Whilst it was agreed that some would be worked to death in permanent concentration camps, the remainder would be killed with the implementation of the Final Solution, which would involve Jews being sent to special killing centres and concentration camps. This would now be the primary method of mass killing, effectively replacing killing units such as the Einsatzgruppe mobile death squads' campaign of murder through Ukraine.

Although the continuation of mass murder across Ukraine would not be so extensive and widespread as it had been in 1941, the country would remain shrouded in a policy of extermination and recrimination, including the Einsatzgruppen carrying out numerous mass executions. In January 1942, a company of Tatar volunteers was set up in Simferopol under the command of Einsatzgruppe II. This company participated in frequent anti-Jewish manhunts and murder actions in the rural regions. The Germans were determined to remove every hostile element from Ukraine so that the country could be self-governed without the worry of what they deemed enemies of the state. In preparation for this, the Nazis had already established what was known as the Reichskommissariat Ukraine, or Reich Commissariat of Ukraine. This administration was governed by the Reich Ministry for the Occupied Territories and headed by Alfred Rosenberg. It was established purely to constitute a territory independent of Russia with a temporary Ukrainian government under German political, economic and military control. Hitler wanted the Reichskommissariat Ukraine established in order to weaken Ukrainian aspirations for independence. He also envisaged the post-war unification of Ukraine with the territory of the German Reich. However, in his eyes, most Ukrainians were considered unfit for Germanisation and he was determined to either eradicate them in concentration camps or resettle them beyond the Urals to make room for German colonists. In the event, Hitler was unable to encourage many Germans to colonise Ukraine. Despite determined plans, only a few villages were cleared of their Ukrainian inhabitants and populated with Germans. Instead, Ukraine would continue to be subjected to racial discrimination, killings and widespread collaboration with the Ukrainian nationalists.

Operating alongside the Einsatzgruppen, Ukrainian nationalist units and numerous police battalions were involved in various types of massacre, including Police Battalion 133, which participated in the killing of Jews and partisans. Between October 1941 and the summer of 1942, it is estimated that some 15,000 victims were killed by this particular battalion alone. The battalion was involved in massacres in Stanisławów, Kolomyia, Deliatyn, Jaremcze, Drohovycz, Bolekhiv, and other towns, leaving communities destroyed. They also assisted in the final liquidation of the ghettos and prepared transports to Belzec extermination camp in 1942 from Kolomyia and Stanisławów.

Through 1942, more police battalions were given 'special tasks' on the Eastern Front, including in Ukraine, which involved a variety of duties, mainly killing actions and mopping up the rear areas. Together with Einsatzgruppe units, auxiliaries, local police and Ukrainian nationalists, they continued roaming the countryside, searching as they advanced and wiping out as many Soviet and Jewish communities as possible. Many of the killings, especially in Ukraine, were undertaken by fellow Ukrainians commanded by German officers. Throughout 1942, extermination actions continued. There were still widespread slaughters in various towns and villages, but generally, the concept of murder was now shifting. There was a slow transition from mass shootings to killing by gas, but there were still ongoing executions, especially during round-ups for transportation to the extermination camps or in the reduction of ghettos. Yet, in spite of the change of policy, Einsatzgruppe units were still roaming in the rear areas and undertaking various killing actions. On 6 April in the town of Pyriatin, 1,600 Jews were murdered.

Police units and civil militia established by the Nazi authorities continued to play a prominent role of collaboration with the Nazis in Ukraine, participating not only in the genocide of many of the Jewish population but also in the killing of Soviet prisoners. They were also involved in the murder of Ukrainian and Jewish civilians, such as the killing of 3,000 people in the village of Kortelisy in September 1942. Other killings continued across Ukraine as the German Army secured more territory. The German military advance had led to the destruction or partial destruction of the country, with much of its industrial base in ruins. Yet, the German triumph over Ukraine would be short-lived, as military reverses in southern Russia would change the outcome on the Eastern Front for ever.

By February 1943, the front had moved almost 200 miles west in less than ten weeks, threatening German forces in eastern Ukraine and the strategically important city of Kharkov. As German units retreated, they were instructed under Hitler's orders to create 'a zone of annihilation'. Everything was to be destroyed in their wake and killings of the local population continued.

A photograph taken of Ukrainian peasants in 1942. Some 2.2 million people were taken from Ukraine to Germany and forced to work in various armaments factories or other industries for the war effort. These workers were known as *Ostarbeiter*, or 'eastern workers'.

A policeman on the left and a Wehrmacht officer converse with a local Ukrainian peasant in the Dnipropetrovsk region. In the spring of 1942, a special killing unit, known as Sonderkommando Plath, was installed by the security police in the region.

A German propaganda photography unit has taken a picture of a group of Ukrainian peasants. During 1942, the German and Ukrainian police, with the assistance of the Wehrmacht, undertook a number of security actions.

(**Above**) Order Police can be seen in an unidentified Ukrainian town. Although various policies for the method of mass killings were changing, there were still episodes of unrestrained terror in Ukraine. These included operations comprising numerous police battalions assisting Ukrainian Auxiliary Police and Einsatzgruppen in a series of widespread cleansing actions across the country. *(Yad Vashem)*

(**Opposite, above**) A group of Ukrainian men have been rounded up by the Order Police. A number of police units were responsible for anti-partisan actions, where they would be arrested and either shot or hanged. These successful actions earned the respect of many of the Order Police commanders and some police officers were awarded with medals and other decorations. *(Yad Vashem)*

(**Opposite, below**) Ukrainian women and men have been publically hanged during what the Order Police termed anti-partisan operations. Some of these so-called partisan actions were loosely termed and they were often no more than victims being targeted for petty infringements of German local laws. *(Yad Vashem)*

Three photographs showing Russian soldiers who had been held in a camp before being forced into a field and executed. During German operations through Ukraine, Soviet prisoners of war, civilians and Jews were routinely selected and shot on the spot. Often those responsible for the murders termed these killings acts of revenge for resistance in combat by alleged insurgents. There were numerous stories of massacres where soldiers gave fictitious reasons for these barbaric killings. *(Yad Vashem)*

(**Above**) German soldiers arrest a Ukrainian man, who is being escorted to a ghetto. By early 1942, the Reichskommissariat Ukraine began creating ghettos in the western part of the country. These ghettos varied greatly. Some consisted of a few fenced-off buildings, whilst others comprised Jews being held in towns where they were forcibly moved into a small quarter that was declared a ghetto, but was often not fenced in or even guarded. However, in the eastern part of the country, the situation was slightly different because most of the police units had killed almost all of the Jewish inhabitants following the Nazi occupation. *(Yad Vashem)*

(**Opposite, above**) A member of the Order Police converses with two Ukrainian men in a village. Over 11,000 members of the Order Police entered Russia and Ukraine in the wake of the German invasion. These units continued to carry out 'special tasks' in 1942 behind the Russian front and each police regiment was often assigned two armoured car and anti-tank platoons. *(Yad Vashem)*

(**Opposite, below**) An Order Police officer executes two Ukrainian men in a field. The two other men who are standing will more than likely meet the same fate. After the war, many Order Police officers claimed not to have been involved in Nazi crimes. *(Yad Vashem)*

A soldier is seen abusing a Ukrainian man. By the spring of 1942, almost no Jews remained alive in German-occupied Right-bank and Left-bank Ukraine. In western Ukraine, the Nazi administration started classifying and organising the surviving Jews for labour. As a result, the murder of women and children intensified. *(Yad Vashem)*

Police Battalion 311 operated in and around Lviv, where it took part in mopping-up actions and the execution of a number of Jews, including assisting in the liquidation of the Lviv Ghetto. However, the battalion was officially responsible for anti-partisan operations. This photograph shows the execution by hanging of members of the Lviv Ghetto *Judenrat* (Jewish council), 1942. *(Yad Vashem)*

Order Police, supported by Hungarian personnel, round up terrified inhabitants in the Ukrainian town of Chernigov in 1942. The majority of Ukraine's Jews were taken completely by surprise by the swift round-ups, terror and mass murders to which they were subjected. *(Yad Vashem)*

Jews have been force-marched out of a town, probably bound for a labour camp. Order Police can be seen guarding and assisting the transportation. *(Yad Vashem)*

Suspected partisans have been rounded and murdered in a field. A Wehrmacht unit observes the massacre. Often, partisans were publicly hanged as examples, but due to the restrictions on time, many of them were simply rounded up and executed by gunfire. *(Yad Vashem)*

A Ukrainian woman from Kerch mourns the death of her 18-year-old son, murdered by Germans when they were forced to evacuate the city in February 1942. *(Yad Vashem)*

A photograph taken during a 'cleansing' of Jews by German soldiers, who were being assisted by Auxiliary Police militia, in a village in 1942. *(Yad Vashem)*

Leaders of the Ukrainian Insurgent Army and German police. The objective of the Organisation of Ukrainian Nationalists was to drive out occupying powers in a national revolution and set up an independent government headed by a dictator. It was established in October 1942. *(Yad Vashem)*

Kommando der ukrainischen Polizeim
in L e m b e r g
- Abt. I a. -

Tgb.Nr...1853/42

Lemberg, den 27.3.1942.

An das
Kommando der S c h u t z p o l i z e i

im H a u s e

Betr.; Judenaktion am 27.3.1942.-

M E L D U N G

Kommando der ukrainischen Polizei meldet, dass die Juden - aktion am 27.3.1942 nachstehendes Ergebnis gegeben hat:

1. Kommissariat d.ukr.Pol	350	Juden
2. - " - " " "	285	-"-
3. - " - " " "	310	-"-
4. - " - " " "	247	-"-
5. - " - " " "	352	-"-
6. - " - " " "	104	-"-
	insgesamt...........1.648	Juden

die nachgeprüft und in dieser Zahl in die Sobieskischule abgeliefert worden sind.

Beilagen; k e i n e.

- P i t u l e j -
Major der ukrainischen Polizei
und Kommandeur.

Ф.12. оп.1 Д.37, л.15

An operational report for the search and arrest of Jews, signed by the commandant of the Ukrainian Police in Lviv. *(Yad Vashem)*

(**Above**) Order Police officers photographed with an old Jewish gentleman during a cleansing action. In July 1942, approximately 600,000 Jews were still alive in Ukraine. Most of them were murdered between July and November 1942. Almost every day, German police, assisted by Ukrainian Auxiliary Police officers, killed thousands of Jews, especially in August and September 1942.

(**Opposite, above**) An Order Police officer poses for the camera with four dead Ukrainian Jews who have presumably been murdered for escaping from a nearby ghetto. By the summer of 1942, with the Nazi policy of murder changing, there were increased German police raids into ghettos. As a result, Jews tried to escape en masse into woods or to hide in cities and towns. These escapes caused widespread massacres against those who escaped and spread fear among the Ukrainian people, who were terrified of being implicated in assisting the Jewish escapees. During the ghetto liquidations, only a small number of Jews were able to survive by hiding in family camps in the woods, joining the partisans, or going into hiding elsewhere. Some did join the partisans, but even these groups rarely survived. *(Yad Vashem)*

(**Opposite, below**) A group of Russian prisoners of war have been murdered during a forced march. Often, the Ukrainian Auxiliary Police assisted in the escorting of prisoners for transportation to various labour camps. These mobile police units, which were organised at battalion level, were widely engaged in the murder of POWs, Jews and pacification actions in Ukraine, combatting partisans. Subordinated directly under the command of the German Order Police, these police units were responsible for assisting the Einsatzgruppen in various massacres. *(Yad Vashem)*

In the Volhynia region, a German motorcyclist and an infantryman observe a group of murdered men in a field who have apparently been shot by a local police unit. In Volhynia and Podillia (Podolia), nearly all the Jewish inhabitants were murdered. *(Yad Vashem)*

Jews from the Volhynia region being escorted to be murdered. The largest massacres occurred in the Volhynian city of Lutsk on 19–23 August, where nearly 15,000 victims were killed. In early September 1942, 13,500 Jews were killed in Volodymyr-Volynskyi, and in Liuboml on 1–2 October, approximately 10,000 Jews were massacred. *(Yad Vashem)*

(**Above**) Russian prisoners of war are eating the carcass of a horse in the winter of 1942. These prisoners have been recruited to work for the Wehrmacht. On the Eastern Front there were various auxiliary volunteers, nicknamed by the Germans as *Hiwi* (short for *Hilfswilliger*, auxiliary volunteers). Between September 1941 and July 1944, the SS employed thousands of collaborationists, recruited as *Hiwis* directly from the Soviet prisoner of war camps. *(Yad Vashem)*

(**Opposite, above**) Local peasants in western Ukraine in the summer of 1942. By this period of the war, the majority of Jews had been murdered in the western regions.

(**Opposite, below**) This photograph shows members of the community from the Mizocz (Mizoch) Ghetto undressing. Mizocz Ghetto had initially held some 1,700 Jews. On 13 October 1942, on the eve of the ghetto's liquidation, some of the inhabitants rose up against the Germans and were defeated after a short battle. The remaining members of the ghetto community were transported to a ravine in the city of Zdolbuniv, south of Rovno. At the edge of the ravine, the Jews, mostly women and children, were ordered to undress and then were herded down the slope and executed. *(USHMM – Instytut Pamięci Narodowej)*

A German policeman prepares to complete a mass execution of the remaining inhabitants of the Mizocz Ghetto by shooting two Jewish children, who can be seen sitting up, looking very distressed. *(USHMM – Instytut Pamięci Narodowej)*

A German soldier poses for a photograph standing next to a train carrying supplies to the front in the summer of 1942.

A series of images showing a cleansing action in eastern Ukraine and the liquidation of ghettos, which had become policy between 1942 and 1943. A number of buildings have been set on fire. German police units, together with Ukrainian Auxiliary Police, Hungarian troops and forced-labour battalions consisting of Hungarian Jewish men, were implicated in these liquidations. Jews were evacuated and either transported to labour or death camps, or were simply murdered outside the ghettos.

In 1943, with the threat of the Red Army attacking parts of eastern Ukraine, the Germans began a scorched-earth policy. In these two photographs, the Germans begin to blow up some of the Ukrainian infrastructure in preparation for a Russian advance.

Stand der Schutzmannschaft am 1. Juli 1943

Generalbezirk	Btl.	Standort	Stärke
Wolh./Podolien	E 101	Starakonstantinow	478
"	W 102	Postave/Ostland	
"	202 poln.		538
"	252 lett.		
Shitomir	E 110	Shitomir	270
"	W 159	Korosten	370
"	Pol.Btl. 25.lett.	Owrutsch	659
Kiew	Pol.Schtz. E 114	Kiew	363
"	W 115	Minsk/Ostland	
"	W 116	Belaja-Zerkow	618
"	W 118	Minsk/Ostland	
"	W 119	Krementschug	238
Nikolajew	W 122	Nikolajew	494
"	E 123	Cherson	643
Dnjepropetrowsk	E 130	Kriwoi-Rog	147
"	W 117 ✓	Kriwoi-Rog	472
" Pol.Btl.Stalag)	F 22 lett.	Saporoshje	368
unter.)	F 268 "	Dnjepropetrowsk	309
Charkow	E 143	Charkow	184
Krim	W 147	Simferopol	419
"	F 148	Karasubasar	417
"	F 149	Bachtschissaraj	384
"	E 150	Jalta	434
"	F 151	Aluschta	394
"	E 154	Simferopol	729
Stalino	W 162	Mariupol	415
"	W 163	Stalino	396
"	W 164	Gorlowka	201

Hier die erbetene Abschrift! Bitte keinen Dank!

Gruß

v. [illegible]mann 25.3.57

Regardless of news of the Red Army being poised to attack the eastern regions of Ukraine, the Nazis were determined to kill as many Jews as possible and formed more Auxiliary Police battalions to ensure this was undertaken. Here is a list of Auxiliary Police battalions formed and/or operating in Ukraine as of 1 July 1943 (not including Galicia). The list does not only include Ukrainian battalions.

German rail cars have been destroyed by a Russian attack during the opening phase of the Battle of the Dnieper in August 1943. This was one of the largest operations of the war and involved some 4 million soldiers. As the Red Army advanced towards the river, the Germans began a widespread scorched-earth policy. Many Jews that had not been killed in these eastern provinces were either shot or transported westwards.

Chapter Four

Aftermath

Even though the war on the Eastern Front in 1943 was becoming progressively worse for the German military, the policy of annihilation of the Jews in Ukraine continued. German authorities were increasingly repressive towards the Ukrainian population, and even the Ukrainian police were reluctant to take part in many of the mass killings, fearing future retribution. Yet by this period of the war, there were still some 100,000 Ukrainian police units that were collaborating with the Nazi authorities, both in Ukraine and across occupied Europe. Many assisted the local authorities, Wehrmacht and SS in mass shootings of Jews, including serving as concentration camp guards. Regardless of the threat of Soviet forces advancing through the eastern regions of Ukraine towards the Dnieper River, there was still widespread coordination between Nazi Ukrainian authorities and Ukrainian nationalists.

Despite their best efforts to destroy the last vestiges of Ukrainian culture, and murder those they considered enemies of the Reich, nothing could prevent the continuing advance of the Red Army through the eastern regions of the country. In order to assist in slowing down the Soviet drive and pacify the local areas, in 1943 the Nazis formed the 14th Waffen-SS Grenadier Division (1st Galician), commonly referred to as the Galicia Division. It was predominantly made up of volunteers with a Ukrainian ethnic background from the area of Galicia. Parts of the division were said to have taken part in a number of massacres. Although the Galicia Division had been formed too late to have participated in the systematic murder of the Jews, it was implicated in the killings at Huta Pieniacka, Pidkamin and Palykorovy. However, the division was almost completely destroyed during the Soviet Lvov–Sandomierz Offensive. The remnants of the division later made up the core of the Liberation Army, which comprised Ukrainian nationalists who wanted to free their own territories from Soviet rule. Units of the Liberation Army were used to pacify the local areas and prevent wholesale surrender to the advancing Russian troops. But the Red Army attacks through Ukraine were so overwhelming that nothing could prevent towns and cities being captured.

As Russian forces were capturing larger areas of eastern Ukraine, the administrative offices for the Reich Commissariat of Ukraine began leaving their various regional offices as German forces implemented a scorched-earth policy by further stripping the areas they had abandoned of anything that could be used by the Soviet war effort. What remained in the wake of the German withdrawal was a country that had endured massive human and material losses. Some 5 to 7 million people had been killed. More than 700 cities and towns and 28,000 villages had been destroyed, with many being completely razed to the ground. Some 10 million people were left displaced or homeless. Only 20 per cent of the industrial enterprises and 15 per cent of agricultural machinery and equipment was salvaged, and the transportation network was massively damaged.

As for the Jewish communities that had thrived in Ukraine before the German policy of terror, it is believed that between 900,000 and 1 million Jews had been murdered as part of the Holocaust in Ukraine. The main accomplices involved in these Ukrainian actions comprised mainly of Einsatzgruppen C and D, Order Police battalions, Russian collaboration, Freiwilligen-Stamm-Division Regiment 3 and 4, known as the Ukrainian Liberation Army, Ukrainian Auxiliary units, and Wehrmacht and SS units.

Following the war, the Soviet authorities tried to diminish the extent of the tragedy that had occurred in Ukraine under Nazi rule. Instead, German documents were accessed to try to piece together what had happened. It was not until the Ukrainian declaration of independence from the Soviet Union in 1991 that a more accurate and devastating picture emerged to increase knowledge of the Holocaust in Ukraine.

Red Army troops liberate Kyiv on 6 November 1943. Soldiers can be seen marching through the liberated streets. Before the German invasion of Ukraine, some 160,000 Jews lived in the city, comprising about 20 per cent of Kyiv's population. Approximately 100,000 Jews fled the city in advance of the Germans. Those Jews who were left behind were subjected to persecution and murder, such as the Babi Yar massacre.

A Russian soldier has been executed during the German withdrawal across the Dnieper River.

Two photographs showing victims murdered at Babi Yar. Before the German authorities retreated from Kyiv ahead of the Red Army offensive of 1944, Paul Blobel, who had commanded the massacre two years earlier, ordered *Sonderaktion 1005* (Special Action 1005) to conceal all traces of the mass murder. Many thousands of bodies were exhumed and burned in the surrounding farmland. However, there were so many bodies that not all the evidence could be hidden. *(Yad Vashem)*

The first of two photographs taken by a Russian photography unit. On the Eastern Front by 1944, Russian forces were advancing at speed and driving their powerful units across the Dnieper River westwards towards the Polish border. During their advance, they came across numerous killing sites, execution pits, labour and concentration camps, and piles of naked victims on horse carts that were in the process of being burnt to conceal their murders. The second photograph shows an open pit with bodies that were being exhumed. However, because the Russian advance was so quick, there was not sufficient time to conceal all of the heinous crimes. *(Yad Vashem)*

Soviet soldiers exhume a mass grave in Lviv. It was confirmed that the mass shooting took place on 18 July 1944 as the Red Army were approaching. *(NARA)*

Appendix One

List of Ukrainian Massacres

The following is a list of the main massacres undertaken by Wehrmacht, Waffen-SS, Einstazgruppen, Order Police, Ukrainian nationalists and Ukrainian Auxiliary Police, Romanian units and local population.

Lviv pogroms (June & July 1941)	Lviv	Einsatzgruppen, Ukrainian nationalists, local crowds	6,000 Jews
Kamianets-Podilskyi massacre (27–28 Aug 1941)	Kamianets-Podilskyi	Wehrmacht units, Ukrainian Auxiliary Police	23,600 Jews
Pavoloch massacre (5 Sep 1941)	Pavoloch	Wehrmacht units	1,500 Jews
Nikolaev massacre (16–30 Sep 1941)	Mykolaiv	Wehrmacht units	35,782 mostly Jews
Babi Yar massacre (29–30 Sep 1941)	Babi Yar	Wehrmacht, Einsazgruppen, police units	33,771 Jews
Berdychiv massacre (5 Oct 1941)	Berdychiv	Wehrmacht, Einsazgruppen, police units	20,000–38,536 Jews
Odesa massacre (22–24 Oct 1941)	Odesa	Wehrmacht, Einsazgruppen, police units, Romanian local crowds	25,000–100,000 Jews
Drobitsky Yar (15 Dec 1941)	Kharkov	Wehrmacht, Einsazgruppen, police units	15,000 Jews
Artemivsk massacre (11 Jan 1942)	Artemivsk (now Bakhmut)	Wehrmacht, Einsazgruppen, police units	1,317–3,000 Jews
Sarny massacre (27–28 Aug 1942)	Sarny	Wehrmacht, Einsazgruppen, police units, Ukrainian Auxilliary Police	14,000–18,000 Jews

Appendix Two

Einsatzgruppe Task Force Ukraine

The list includes Einsatzkommandos, which were a subgroup of the Einsatzgruppen, totalling 3,000 men and usually composed of 500–1,000 personnel.

Einsatzgruppe C
(attached to Army Group South)

Commanders

SS-Brigadeführer und Generalmajor der Polizei Dr Otto Rasch (June–October 1941)
SS-Gruppenführer und Generalleutnant der Polizei Max Thomas (October 1941–29 April 1943)
SS-Standartenführer Horst Böhme (6 September 1943–March 1944)

Einsatzkommando 4a (operated Lviv, Rovno, Lutsk, Pereyaslav, Ivankov, Radomyshl, Lubny, Kyiv, Kursk and Kharkov)

Commanders

SS-Standartenführer Paul Blobel (June 1941–13 January 1942)
SS-Obersturmbannführer Erwin Weinmann (13 January–27 July 1942)
SS-Sturmbannführer Eugen Steimle (August 1942–15 January 1943)
SS-Sturmbannführer Friedrich Schmidt (January–February 1943)
SS-Sturmbannführer Theodor Christensen (March–December 1943)

Einsatzkommando 4b (operated Lviv, Tarnopol, Poltava, Sloviansk, Vinnytsia, Gorlovka and Rostov)

Commanders

SS-Obersturmbannführer Günther Herrmann (June–October 1941)
SS-Obersturmbannführer Fritz Braune (2 October 1941–21 March 1942)
SS-Obersturmbannführer Dr Walter Haensch (March–July 1942)
SS-Obersturmbannführer August Meier (July–November 1942)
SS-Sturmbannführer Friedrich Suhr (November 1942–August 1943)
SS-Sturmbannführer Waldemar Krause (August 1943–January 1944)

Einsatzkommando 5 (operated Lviv, Brody, Dubno, Skvyra and Kyiv)

Commanders

SS-Oberführer Erwin Schulz (June–August 1941)
SS-Sturmbannführer August Meier (September 1941–January 1942)

Einsatzkommando 6 (operated Lviv, Zolochiv, Zhytomyr, Proskurov, Vinnytsia, Kryvyi Rih, Stalino and Rostov)

Commanders

SS-Standartenführer Dr Erhard Kroeger (June–November 1941)
SS-Sturmbannführer Robert Möhr (November 1941–September 1942)
SS-Obersturmbannführer Ernst Biberstein (September 1942–May 1943)
SS-Sturmbannführer Friedrich Suhr (August–November 1943)

Einsatzgruppe D

(attached to the 11th Army and operated in northern Transylvania, Chernivtsi, Kishinev and Crimea area)

Commanders

SS-Gruppenführer und Generalleutnant der Polizei Dr Otto Ohlendorf (June 1941–July 1942)
SS-Brigadeführer und Generalmajor der Polizei Walther Bierkamp (July 1942–March 1943)

Einsatzkommando 10a

Commanders

SS-Oberführer und Oberst der Polizei Heinrich Seetzen (June 1941–July 1942)
SS-Sturmbannführer Dr Kurt Christmann (August 1942–July 1943)

Einsatzkommando 10b

Commanders

SS-Obersturmbannführer Alois Persterer (June 1941–December 1942)
SS-Sturmbannführer Eduard Jedamzik (December 1942–February 1943)

Einsatzkommando 11a

Commanders

SS-Obersturmbannführer Paul Zapp (June 1941–July 1942)
Fritz Mauer (July–October 1942)
SS-Sturmbannführer Dr Gerhard Bast (November–December 1942)
SS-Sturmbannführer Werner Hersmann (December 1942–May 1943)

Einsatzkommando 11b

Commanders

SS-Sturmbannführer Hans Unglaube (June–July 1941)
SS-Obersturmbannführer Bruno Müller (July–October 1941)
SS-Obersturmbannführer Werner Braune (October 1941–September 1942)
SS-Obersturmbannführer Paul Schultz (September 1942–February 1943)

Einsatzkommando 12

Commanders

SS-Obersturmbannführer Gustav Adolf Nosske (June 1941–February 1942)
SS-Sturmbannführer Dr Erich Müller (February–October 1942)
SS-Obersturmbannführer Günther Herrmann (October 1942–March 1943)

Appendix Three

Regular Police Battalions up to July 1942 (Eastern Front)

Numerous Order Police battalions operated in both Russia and Ukraine. Below is a list of main battalions. Some were disbanded, absorbed into new battalions, or recruited into the 4th SS Polizei Division.

Police Battalion 1
Police Battalion 2
Police Battalion 3
Police Battalion 4
Police Battalion 5
Police Battalion 6
Police Battalion 7
Police Battalion 8
Police Battalion 9
Police Battalion 10
Police Battalion 11
Police Battalion 12
Police Battalion 13
Police Battalion 14
Police Battalion 21
Police Battalion 22
Police Battalion 23
Police Battalion 25
Police Battalion 26
Police Battalion 31
Police Battalion 32
Police Battalion 33
Police Battalion 41
Police Battalion 42
Police Battalion 43
Police Battalion 44
Police Battalion 45
Police Battalion 51
Police Battalion 52
Police Battalion 53
Police Battalion 54
Police Battalion 55
Police Battalion 56
Police Battalion 611
Police Battalion 62
Police Battalion 631
Police Battalion 64
Police Battalion 65
Police Battalion 66
Police Battalion 67
Police Battalion 681
Police Battalion 69
Police Battalion 71
Police Battalion 721
Police Battalion 731
Police Battalion 74
Police Battalion 81
Police Battalion 82
Police Battalion 83
Police Battalion 84
Police Battalion 85
Police Battalion 207
Police Battalion 208
Police Battalion 209
Police Battalion 210
Police Battalion 251
Police Battalion 252
Police Battalion 253
Police Battalion 254
Police Battalion 256
Police Battalion 301
Police Battalion 302
Police Battalion 303
Police Battalion 304
Police Battalion 305
Police Battalion 306
Police Battalion 307
Police Battalion 308
Police Battalion 309
Police Battalion 310
Police Battalion 311
Police Battalion 312
Police Battalion 313
Police Battalion 314
Police Battalion 315
Police Battalion 316
Police Battalion 317
Police Battalion 318
Police Battalion 319
Police Battalion 320
Police Battalion 321
Police Battalion 322
Police Battalion 323
Police Battalion 324
Police Battalion 325

Appendix Four

Nazi Collaborators in Ukraine

Schutzmannschaft (Ukraine Auxiliary Police)

Ukrainian Schutzmannschaft battalions

9th, 50th, 114th, 115th, 116th, 117th, 118th, 201st
(participated in anti-partisan operations in Ukraine)

Ukrainian volunteers in the German armed forces

Nachtigall Battalion (Nightingale Battalion)
Battalion Ukrainische Gruppe Roland (Roland Battalion)
Freiwilligen-Stamm-Division (Volunteer Depot Division)

Ukrainian Insurgent Army

Northern Operational Group

Regions: Volhynia, Polissia

Military District: Turiv

Commander: Major Rudyj
Squads: Bohun, Pomsta Polissja, Nalyvajko

Military District: Zahrava

Commander: Ptashka (Sylvester Zatovkanjuk)
Squads: Konovaletsj, Enej, Dubovyj, Oleh

Military District: Volhynia-South

Commander: Bereza
Squads: Kruk, H

Western Operational Group

Regions: Halychyna, Bukovina, Zakarpattia, Zakerzonia

Military District: Lysonja

Commander: Major Hrim, V.
Kurins: Holodnojarci, Burlaky, Lisovyky, Rubachi, Bujni, Holky

Military District: Hoverlja

Commander: Major Stepovyj (from 1945, Major Hmara)
Kurins: Bukovynsjkyj, Peremoha, Hajdamaky, Huculjskyj, Karpatsjkyj

Military District: Black Forest

Commander: Colonel Rizun-Hrehit (Mykola Andrusjak)

Kurins: Smertonosci, Pidkarpatsjkyj, Dzvony, Syvulja, Dovbush, Beskyd, Menyky
Military District: Makivka
Commander: Major Kozak
Kurins: Ljvy, Bulava, Zubry, Letuny, Zhuravli, Bojky of Chmelnytsjkyj, Basejn
Military District: Buh
Commander: Colonel Voronnyj
Kurins: Druzhynnyky, Halajda, Kochovyky, Perejaslavy, Tyhry, Perebyjnis
Military District: Sjan
Commander: Orest
Kurins: Vovky, Menyky, Kurin of Ren, Kurin of Eugene

Southern Operational Group
Regions: Khmelnytskyi Oblast, Zhytomyr Oblast, southern region of Kyiv Oblast, southern regions of Ukraine, and especially in cities Odesa, Kryvyi Rih, Dnipropetrovsk, Mariupol, Donetsk.
Military District: Cholodnyj Jar
Commander: Kost
Kurins: Sabljuk, Dovbush
Military District: Umanj
Commander: Ostap
Kurins: Dovbenko, Buvalyj, Andrij-Shum.
Military District: Vinnytsia
Commander: Jasen
Kurins: Storchan, Mamaj, Burevij

SS Division Galicia
14 Waffen Grenadier Division der SS (galizische Nr. 1) (14th Waffen Grenadier Division of the SS (1st Galician)